Questions from Outer Space

Questions from Outer Space

poems

Diane Thiel

Red Hen Press | *Pasadena, CA*

Book design by Daniela Connor

Library of Congress Cataloging-in-Publication Data

Names: Thiel, Diane, 1967– author.
Title: Questions from outer space: poems / Diane Thiel.
Description: First Edition. | Pasadena, CA: Red Hen Press, [2022]
Identifiers: LCCN 2021042550 (print) | LCCN 2021042551 (ebook) | ISBN
    9781636280271 (trade paperback) | ISBN 9781636280288 (epub)
Subjects: LCGFT: Poetry.
Classification: LCC PS3570.H4418 Q47 2022 (print) | LCC PS3570.H4418
    (ebook) | DDC 811/.54—dc23
LC record available at https://lccn.loc.gov/2021042550
LC ebook record available at https://lccn.loc.gov/2021042551

Publication of this book has been made possible in part through the generous financial
support of Dana and Mary Gioia and the University of New Mexico.

The National Endowment for the Arts, the Los Angeles County Arts Commission, the Ah-
manson Foundation, the Dwight Stuart Youth Fund, the Max Factor Family Foundation,
the Pasadena Tournament of Roses Foundation, the Pasadena Arts & Culture Commission
and the City of Pasadena Cultural Affairs Division, the City of Los Angeles Department of
Cultural Affairs, the Audrey & Sydney Irmas Charitable Foundation, the Meta & George
Rosenberg Foundation, the Albert and Elaine Borchard Foundation, the Adams Family
Foundation, Amazon Literary Partnership, the Sam Francis Foundation, and the Mara W.
Breech Foundation partially support Red Hen Press.

First Edition
Published by Red Hen Press
www.redhen.org

ACKNOWLEDGMENTS

My thanks to the editors of the following journals and publications, in which these poems first appeared, a few in different versions:

2River: "Astronaut Training," "Assimilation," "Field Notes from the Biolayer"; *American Journal of Poetry*: "Hippocampus (Elliptical Scans from Space)," "Living with Aliens," "Remotely"; *Belfield Literary Review* (Ireland): "How They Arrived"; *Birmingham Poetry Review*: "Listening in Deep Space"; *Brilliant Corners: A Journal of Jazz and Literature*: "Pantoum on a Paper Moon"; *Broad River Review*: "Interplanetary Spelling Bee"; *Burden of the Beholder* (The Press at Colorado College): "The First Sea"; *Catamaran*: "Learning to Breathe"; *Cathexis Northwest Press*: "Tritina in the Time of the Machine"; *Change Seven*: "Under the Rug"; *The Common*: "On Foot"; *Cordella*: "This Old Thing"; *Crosswinds*: "So Much Depends"; *Dappled Things*: "The Typewriter"; *The Dark Horse* (Scotland): "Baby Out with the Bathwater," "Changing Reality," "Short Subjects with Long Titles (Epigrams on Art, Poetics and Philosophy)," "So Much Depends"; *Delmarva Review*: "Zero Hour"; *The Festival Review*: "Time in the Wilderness"; *First Things*: "Outback"; "Spaceship with Saint Giovannino," "Sticks and Stones"; *Havik*: "The Slide"; *The Hopkins Review*: "Just Before Dawn," "Sleeping Dogs"; *The Hudson Review*: "Hiatus," "Notice from Another Dimension," "The Factory (Questions from Outer Space)," "The Multiverse," "Under the Lawrence Tree"; *Library of Congress National Book Festival* (recording, webcast): "Counting Two"; *Louisiana Literature: A Review of Literature and the Humanities*: "Circle in the Sand," "Measure by Time," "One Early Morning"; *Malasaña*: "Birth Announcement," "Elemental Trail"; *Notre Dame Review*, Issue 52, Summer 2021: "Kummerspeck," "Time Won't Do It"; *Novus Literary Arts Journal*: "Southern Cross"; *Orange Blossom Review*: "Isn't poetry all about perfection?"; *La Piccioletta Barca*: "Three Seasons"; *Plainsongs*: "Kwick Assess"; *Poemcafe* (Korea; translated into Korean): "Carousel"; *Poetry Porch*: "Giant Children," "Questions from Four Dimensions"; *Prairie Schooner*: "Letters from La Paz"; *Prime Number Magazine*: "The Farthest Side"; *Provincetown Arts*: "Babes in the Wood," "Love-Spinning"; *Rattle*: "High Noon at the Remote Corral"; *Red Rock Review*: "In the Mirror"; *The Sewanee Review*: "Recovering the Lost"; *The Same*: "Three Surrealist Women and the Skins of an Orchestra"; *South Florida Poetry Journal*: "Haiku Petroglyphs," "Swamp Roses"; *Sunbeams*: "Changing Reality"; *Sutterville Review*: "Navigating the Questions"; *Taos Journal of International Poetry and Art*: "In the Rain," "Library of Veria"; *Terrain*: "Questions of Time and Direction"; *THINK: A Journal of Poetry, Fiction, and Essays*: "Finding Home"; *Waterproof* (O, Miami; Jai-Alai Books): "Planting Cape Florida, Key Biscayne"; and *West Trade Review*: "Expendable."

I also appreciate the editors and associations which presented the following awards and/or featured my poems: "The Farthest Side" tied for Second Place in the annual Prime Number Magazine Award for Poetry and was also nominated for a Pushcart Prize. "The First Sea" won the Journey Daily Poetry Contest and was featured on their podcast. "Under the Rug" was a Finalist for the 50th New Millennium Award for Poetry. "Changing Reality" was a Finalist for the Joan Ramseyer Memorial Poetry Award. A selection of poems including "On Foot," "Measure by Time," and "Under the Rug" was a Finalist for the Princemere Poetry Prize. "Haiku Petroglyphs" was featured on *Poetic Routes: An Interactive Cartography*. "Love-spinning" and "Southern Cross" were featured in *Sparks of Calliope*. "Counting Two" and "Three Seasons" were featured in *MacQueen's Quinterly*. "Recovering the Lost" was featured in *Mediterranean Poetry*. "Counting Two," "The First Sea," and "Learning to Breathe" have been set to music by composer Dale Trumbore. In addition, I extend thanks to the NEA for the NEA International Literature Award and to PEN for the PEN Translation Award which helped fund travel in connection with some of these poems.

For Dylan, Christabel,
Aria, and Alexander,
who continually bring me
new visions of the world

Contents

III
The Farthest Side

IV
Time in the Wilderness

*Then the doors of perception open slightly
and the other time appears, the real one
we were searching for without knowing it:
the present, the presence.*

—Octavio Paz

*Some, and I'm one,
Wander sitting still . . .
Walk out when you want, choose
Your bread and your company.*

—Marie Ponsot

I

Questions of Time and Direction

In which language does rain fall
over tormented cities? . . .

What did the tree learn from the earth
to be able to talk with the sky?

—Pablo Neruda

Just Before Dawn

The frog in between stages
catches our attention early on.
Sometimes a photo from
a certain year of change appears,
and we find something
nearly forgotten.

Every day our cells renew,
every ten years entirely,
in ways we study but don't
completely understand,
until one day we notice
something has happened.

We might still look the same
that morning, but all
our cells must have finally
crossed over, the last ones
in the night, in the hours
just before dawn.

Measure by Time

after Vladimir Kush's painting, *Open World*

The children can easily fit themselves inside
the toy that fits inside a pocket,
shifting size and shape throughout the day
and then expanding into their dreams.
The world opens through the fairy tale,
the counterpoint to climb, holding onto
the music, note by note, measure by time.
It might be entirely new, or a memory
we have already held in our hands.
Existence as we know it, the song
wound tight and coiled,
is about to expand.

From one angle, it might look like
a simple combination of a container
and a sphere. Such a small space compared
to the great expanse, but holding more
than the usual flotsam of the stars.
The volcano is smoking and sure
to change things, shift the plates and continents.
Something is arriving.
All the elements could come together
at any moment, and the planets in the distance
are watching closely
to see what happens next.

Remotely

In the culture of Remotely, things were heading that way
long before the virus. Once they could remotely
operate things, every home in Remotely had one.
The young and the old fought over who would remotely control
their evenings. Some remotely raised their children,
absent or remotely present even when they were there.
Some things taken for granted were harder to do remotely.
Procreation was possible, but remotely desirable
once it became that clinical, remotely transferring cells
and later cell phones, once they all only remotely connected.

We have observed them remotely for years, as they put up walls,
charted all their remotely comprehensible conflicts, and decided
when in Remotely, we would do as the Remotelians,
keep to our screens, and only get remotely involved.

Hippocampus (Elliptical Scans from Space)

The seahorse in the brain
appears to be in charge
of memory and navigation.
There is a clear connection
between them, especially
in the way place stirs memory.
They really have no better maps,
though they persist in printing them,
when they could simply access
the cognitive ones already built in.
The brain will recognize certain action
potentials, but often fail to act.
Declarative memory should allow
some to speak that choose not to,
but this is likely hard-learned
and hard-wired by some
intense learning event.

The seahorse is sensitive to conflict
and learns to navigate carefully
when there is uncertainty of reward
or punishment, and this strongly affects
decision-making. The theta rhythm
is familiar, the way tempos like walking
and the deep recharging connect
memory to a multitude of applications.
The storage of the memories
is in a different segment. They often
make the transfer in the night.

The hippocampus is not to be confused
with the hippopotamus,
as one researcher did in 1779, and others
followed suit (another common trait)
before the error was controlled.
Our studies, though, have found
that many might, in fact,

have such a semi-aquatic ungulate
residing in the brain, quietly
munching away, seemingly calm,
but also dangerous and unpredictable,
huge for such an area, unmoving
and eventually removing other functions,
making it harder to accept and retain
new information. We might
reasonably refer to this condition
as hippopotamus of the brain.

(with apologies to the hippopotamus)

The Factory (Questions from Outer Space)

From out here it appears
to be one big factory.
I am not talking about the smoke.
That's in another report.

I can't really figure them out.
They finally find the way to create
a wonderful tool to connect the world,
and within a few years,
it is also a production line
selling bodies, bets, packaged ideas
with no nutrition. I've read the labels.

They plug themselves into it because
that is what they did yesterday.
Some inject it directly with a needle.
Some barely speak to each other,
communicating only via the suggested
words of the system.

Now it is a two-faced swindle especially used
to deface—to catch and eviscerate
someone who speaks an unpopular truth.
The system purports that speech is free,
but it is clear that speech can be costly.
There is a sliding scale on freedom, and for some,
a steep learning curve to get that lesson.

But we shouldn't be surprised.
They've built these centers all over
that had such promise
and turned them also into factories
where the new arrivals each year
climb on the assembly lines,
fixed tracks, forming what to think.

The main drive is to make you sign on and then
stay on the learning platform and keep on clicking,
to make sure all the products emerge
from the same mold, with the same formations.
This must be something other than what was intended.
Why would they train such an incredibly free brain
to conform to such small dimensions?

But to end the report
on a hopeful note,
and believe me, they do need one,
every now and then I notice
someone walks out of the factory,
battered, scarred, but still standing
and looks up at the stars
with a surprising question,
trying to find a different answer.

Questions of Time and Direction

Why do they continually move in the opposite
direction from where they are looking?
It may have something to do with the way life
begins for them. While in the ground, they add flesh
over time until they are ready to leave the box,
or else they emerge fully formed from the ashes.

Almost immediately, they begin offering food
out of their bodies. They draw liquids and gases
from their machines to present item after item in a system
that fits it all perfectly into the Earth, in reserved holes,
the coal placed in storage via the replenishing mines,
the oil by way of wells, deposited deep into the land.

When did they become so generous? Giving everything
they have over time to collection facilities,
offering hides and fur to cover other beings, bringing
valuable ivory from homes to affix teeth and tusks.
They are even assisting in the creation of new species
at a more rapid rate than we have witnessed anywhere,

species they never even knew could exist.
How can they do it so quickly?
Effect so much change in a single generation.
Forests appear almost instantaneously,
storing so much medicine, so many answers,
and assuring the oxygen they need to breathe.

After a crash on the shore, the waves in their oceans
unroll out to sea, sometimes moving objects
toward places as far as the massive trash vortex.
Like the currents, the ships, countries and even one hand
or another gather the debris from the patches, piece by piece,
the chemicals sucked in through tubes.

They do this collecting so regularly, they must
recognize the essential nature of their actions.
They seem to forecast the world using art,
drawing it in through brushes or other tools,
colors bottled into containers, notes into instruments,
words into devices or a simple pen.

Perhaps most vital to their continued existence
is the way they are regularly removing the toxins
from the atmosphere at a rapid pace, enhancing the layer
of protection that surrounds them. Unlike us, they need
a planet to exist. They are busy evolving their nature,
clearly necessary for their long-term survival.

So forward-thinking and such good stewards.
But we do have some conflicting data, based on other reports
from a closer perspective. It is possible that, like Venus,
their neighbor, at some point their sphere began turning
backwards on its axis. Time sometimes reverses,
depending on where we are in one universe or another.

Since we are no longer expanding out here,
at this distance from which we are observing,
we have begun to question if such a reversal
could be affecting our readings, if the way
we perceive them at this point might involve
a crucial question of time and direction.

Field Notes from the Biolayer

It seems to require extreme conditions.
Some do listen to the early alarms, but many will ignore
all evidence until the water rises above their heads.

As the virus sweeps, and they are forced
to rely on the virtual world, some begin to realize
what they had been missing, how much they miss touch,

the sound of voices and music not filtered through machines.
We have always found the music to be curious,
the way they use it to connect,

the way some sing to get through things.
Though I have seen enough not to be naive,
the possibilities are staggering.

More are recognizing the way their world is connected
within and also beyond—the rivers, the oceans, the air—
the lovely layer that makes their existence possible.

Spatial Equations

"The math confirms this biosphere
is highly similar to ours."

      "And the probes postulate their digits
      determined their digits."

"Yes. They add and multiply,
then subtract and divide."

      "Can they simplify?"

"Probably. But they generally
complicate things."

      "Highly irrational.
      And the zero?"

"It determines everything. But some
will always translate it to nothing."

Listening in Deep Space

We've always been out looking for answers,
telling stories about ourselves,
searching for connection, choosing
to send out Stravinsky and whale song
which, in translation, might very well be
our undoing instead of a welcome.

We launch satellites, probes, telescopes
unfolding like origami, navigating
geomagnetic storms, major disruptions.
Rovers with spirit and perseverance
mapping the unknown. We listen
through large arrays adjusted eagerly

to hear the news that we are not alone.
Considering the history at home,
in houses, across continents, oceans,
even in quests armed with good intentions,
what one seeker has done to another—
what will we do when we find each other?

Navigating the Questions

When my daughter came to me with a homework passage
from *Silent Spring*, asking about DDT,
I didn't quite know how to tell her what I had seen

with my own eyes, decades after the U.S. ban,
the DDT used for fishing in Colombia, the people sprinkling it
in the water for the fish to rise to the surface, belly up.

The companies had sent it down there instead,
if the mind can wrap around that.
It will all come back to us, in one way or another.

Some seasons of questions harder than others—
hurricanes, political disasters, a continent on fire.
When the virus shut down even the schools,

I told my children I didn't know how long it would
really be—that it had never happened in my life.
I was thinking about the virus when I tried to answer,

but I couldn't stop thinking about the oceans connecting us
and the fish, all the fish between us, and the way we still act
as though it is all separate. Our lives on this planet

so intertwined, it will all come back to us,
and our children will have to navigate
the questions we leave them.

So Much Depends

So much today
depended on the tracks,
the thick groove of a wheel on the trail
where I always see prints—deer, bobcat,
sometimes bear scat.

So much depended on the wheelbarrow
on the side of the trail
that changed the image forever in an instant
when they came for it.

I had the feeling not much would depend on what I said.
I asked when the season would end.
I said to be careful, that kids took this trail all day,
said how tame the deer are here, so unafraid.
And then I just said—don't take too many.

So much depends
on how much we take,
how much the wheelbarrows hold.

Walking that long way home,
so much depending
on the possibly indistinguishable crunch
of my feet, the light fading,
the night coming so early these days.

I found myself saying lines of poems out loud
to make another sound. I had done that before,
once when a pack of coyotes howling felt too close,
and once when there was word of a bear nearby,
so much depending on whether
we came too close to each other.

But today I did it, maybe to announce
my humanity, so the hunters wouldn't
accidentally take me out.
But as I heard my own voice
in the oncoming night,
I also thought hard about how much
depended on that, my humanity,
and what that meant,
even as I said it out loud
in the falling light.

Expendable

My grandmothers, in different ways,
on different continents, lost everything they knew,
were dispossessed of home and started over.
One grandmother was lucky that she sewed
a perfect stich and made just enough to live
and raise her children on her own.
The other washed the West Virginia coal dust
from her husband, who died too young,
the land and his body hollowed out together,
and washed it from six sons before she sent them
off to war when they were called.

My grandmothers took what work they could find
and came of age around the time when the radium girls
in the U.S. Radium factories, some the sole support of families,
dipped their implements, painted the watch dials, while
instructed to point the tips of the brushes with their lips.
Lip, dip, paint, so as not to waste time or the radium,
while behind the door, the lab technicians were given
gloves and protective clothing. The girls joked with each other
and laughed about the way their bodies glowed at night,
before their teeth fell out, and bone by bone,
their bodies decayed.

How unthinkable the history seems today, even as we
watch it happen, in the way our actions decide
who or what is now
expendable.

Time Won't Do It

We expect too much of time,
give it mythical powers,
believe a certain set of hours,
days or years will be the salve
to solve it all. We treat it
like an oracle, believing
time will tell, expecting
time to heal because
our sayings say it will.
We expect time to do our
dirty work, clean up after us.
But time won't do it by itself.

Not without us, won't really heal
the wounds, will only cover them,
like geologic sands might
sift into a smooth surface
for a time, until some event
or seemingly small shift
unearths the fissure underneath,
sometimes when we least
expect it. Over time,
time might help,
but time sure won't
do it by itself.

Sticks and Stones

Some say it like a charm
in the face of words heavy as stone,
or a riddle of subtle pebbles thrown,
each sticking point like a firearm.
As if the saying would erase the harm.
Raging fire or cold as ice, we've known
too well where words can send us.
Words can cut us to the bone
and even end us.

In the Rain

As if the rain could fill the spaces in
her heart, she liked to go out in the rain,
walk like the wind the trees make when they move.
That is what she believed when she was little,
that the trees made the wind,
that they would blow up a big storm some time

and carry her away, on the back of a giant bird.
And she would see mountains and never hear
words again. She had grown afraid of words,
what could be done to them, how they could be
slaughtered with the change of a syllable,
cooked and served and eaten in one swallow.

As if that swallow could fill you like rain
fills the rivers, fills the trees.

Babes in the Wood

The last place I want to go
is back to that dark wood.
Why would I take you there?

Yet here I am, exactly where
I needed not to be,
where words have always carried me.

I wish I could un-learn
the spell to spin free
all the caged words.

I dreamt you stuck your finger through
the bars—the flesh and bone
rose-red, thin, curved like a thorn

How many ways to lose you
How many ways to lose
before you're even born.

Three Seasons

When I first heard the story, I was Persephone,
feet in the blossoms, oblivious,
on the edge of another world.

Once the pomegranate broke on my own doorstep,
I found the summer, but too soon became Demeter,
searching for my child, calling into that underworld,

thinking of the third season, harvest or loss,
that might arrive before its time
and take away the world.

Hiatus

It would be easy to say it was Tahiti.
Some months turned into years.
The sand was warm. The children
swam like fish and grew
like stories do.
There was no cancer at the age of six,
no surreal cruelty that in tandem
showed its double face.
No toxic cocktail of the two.

Hiatus can sometimes mean
a claim for freedom. Time.
An interruption in a chain
of events. In logic, a gap in reasoning.
But in the body and especially the heart,
it can also be a chasm,
an opening that let too much through at once,
that left a tear in the continuum
seemingly forever,
that all the coconut threads of mythical Tahiti
still can't sew back together.

II

Notice from Another Dimension

I was saying it to stop
the sensation of falling off
the round, turning world
into cold, blue-black space.

—Elizabeth Bishop

Sleeping Dogs

The problem is
they lie. Ignored,
they tend to cover the floor,
fill the halls, block the door. Eventually,
there is not a decent spot to put your foot.
They have gathered here for years, taking root,
seeming to be sleeping. You have to walk gingerly
to get past them all. Here and there avoid a tail. Avoid
the growl inside the nightmare. Make your way, step
by careful
side-step.
But if the door is blocked, you might still get
out whatever window
isn't covered yet.
Some of us, historically,
are good at this.
Some of us learned early
how to squeeze through such
tight-lipped passages.

Baby Out with the Bathwater

When something needs some cleaning up,
we've been known to fill the tub,
begin to scrub away, though
one hopes for a gentler touch
if that something
is a baby.
The warning is depicted in a woodcut,
a *Far Side* of the sixteenth century
that shows the baby upside down,
hands flailing, being tossed out
with the water from the tub.
One would think it unlikely
to forget that there's a baby
when we begin with some
purposeful, surely harmless
cleaning up, but some
persist in ending up
forgetting that, regardless.

KwickAssess

With KwickAssess, you'll do much less,
eliminate the need to guess
about a work of art, a mate,
an applicant, a candidate.
Our algorithm takes the stress

of choice away. So why obsess?
Adjust the software to address
hardware beliefs, remove debate.
With KwickAssess, you'll do much less!

Or click for KwickAssessExpress.
Side effects include gray matter loss
of self-reliance catatonic state
The diamond upgrade now! Don't wait!
The fastest pathway to success—
Do less—with KwickAssessExpress!

The Multiverse

We started talking about the multiverse
before the twentieth century, a different way
of making sense, acknowledging
the changeability and indifference.
Science opening up the notion
of one self turning left
while another is driven to turn right,
a new conundrum of freedom and constraint.
Despite the theories, most of us
still hold on to the universe
as the largest thing we can imagine.

But sometimes I watch that other self
from a different angle on the multiversity,
slide down that other choice, what I might
have said instead, in that room of dry twigs,
gasoline in the corner, and so many matches,
then watch myself continue along
that low road for a while, too long at times,
wondering how that would all turn out.
My doppelgänger grinning in the distance,
waving from what looks like a getaway car,
moving out of sight to live out a half-life
I can never keep track of.
And really, who knows I didn't
take that turn? Who knows that isn't
a reality? It is certainly more satisfying
than this silence.

We usually have more than two choices,
infinitely more in this pluralistic multiverse,
as Oppenheimer put it when his work opened boxes

without opening them, when he elaborated on
one unfortunate cat, or a lucky one,
while another self exploded and ended
far more than his better self
would ever have agreed to
or intended.

Under the Rug

It started with the dirt. A few swishes of the broom
and no one noticed. And then some broken glass
that crunched underneath as anyone passed.
But still no one paid much attention.
Then there were some files no one wanted
to handle. Followed by the flies and rotting garbage.
Chicken bones and feathers. Apparently,
people can overlook anything.
All this led to the rolling under
of the grenade,
with the pin still in, at least. People did avoid that spot,
taking extra care on that frayed and unraveling end.
Through all this reshuffling, the elephant
had been sitting quietly in the corner,
trying to remain inconspicuous, until one day
they decided it had to go under too.
The elephant handlers arrived in suits and ties
and quickly learned that the elephant
would not go quietly under the rug, but
        resisted fiercely
                and started trumpeting down the hallway,
            knocking over tables,
              chairs and bookcases,
                    dragging the rug, exposing everything
      for just long enough to create a bit of shock—
before the rug handlers quickly put back the rug
on top of everything,
left the elephant alone, watching from the corner,
and everyone went back to the charade,
to this day especially avoiding
the spot
with the grenade.

The Slide

Sometimes to avoid
conflict, we might let it slide.
Some of us, over time, have developed
quite a smooth side, that will slide the muck thrown
down off of us, leaving barely a trace to an outside eye.

But eventually, it becomes clear
that not everything can slide.
Some things are just too big,
and if we try, it would crush the slide,
rupture a fissure in the ground.
No one would know
how to fix such a deep rift,
heading all the way down to an abyss.
Clearly, at least to the discerning eyes,
such a slide would be too dangerous.

The hazard tape wrapped
all around the slide
would become a permanent
fixture in the park.

So if I can't let this one slide
into that chasm, I know I have to speak,
but from too much experience, I also know
        where this could slide, regardless—
                what objection can trigger, with debris
                        having collected here for years.
                                Hard to watch, but easy to predict
                                        the mud flow that will follow,
                                                taking everything with it.

Tritina in the Time of the Machine

In nearly every pocket, a small, methodical machine,
but the world still unprepared for the systematic replicating
deep inside cells. The reckoning strand trying to come alive

using the hosts, chosen to copy, repeat, bring them alive
on the most basic scale. A sharp spike of the stealthy machine,
just waiting for another opening, ready to be replicating

everything it needs. At first, we barely notice the replicating,
from exo-brain to endo-coding. Some neurons only half-alive
in any given decision anyway, and over time mostly machine,

the machine grinding on, replicating its meaning of alive.

Assimilation

Trying to write something about
Borges and his dystopian purifiers,
but living a few different realities at once,
I keep thinking about the Borg.

After the screen, their image persists,
the implants, maturation chambers,
the hive so alien and familiar.
The perfection.

I wanted the poem to be funny, wry at least,
carry its own kind of meta-resistance,
but as I find myself saying out loud in the house,
There is nothing funny about the Borg.

My twelve-year-old, as usual, pulls me out
of that futile spiral, pointing out, *Well, it's funny
that they always say the same thing.*
They do—despite all that math, all those letters,

consuming all those libraries of information,
all those possible ways of solving problems.
It *is* funny, but also terrifying
to always hear the same thing.

In the Mirror

I confess that I used invisible ink . . . that I write in mirror writing.
—Anna Akhmatova

Silencing	Silencing
falls slowly	slowly falls
first signs	signs first
barely noticeable	noticeable barely
tonight cover of snow	snow of cover tonight
in some cases	cases some in
until poems become code	code become poems until
secret in writing	writing in secret
invisible ink	ink invisible
holding lines in memory	memory in lines holding
smuggling poems	poems smuggling
truth tucked under	under tucked truth
mirrors this too familiar	familiar too this mirrors
place in history	history in place
here again	again here
now silently	silently now
face our records	records our face

Notice from Another Dimension

I had to move, suddenly. I found the crack
in the universe and had to do it.
Things in yours had gone too far
over the edge of reason.
I can still come back and forth.
I suppose I'll keep my job for now.
Collect my paycheck.
I could telecommute, though the reception
might not be the best.
I will probably vote in my old district.
For now we will keep the house.
The moving company was a bit mystified
how it all worked, but together we figured it out.

My kids like it better over here,
and they love the idea
that we found the secret passage
so few know about.
They would rather go to school here,
but they will miss their friends
so we are working on a compromise.

Don't bother looking for us while we're gone.
It's not the type of passageway
just anyone can fit through.
You have to work through a hundred thousand trials
of absurdity to gain entry.
But by then, I could even bring my family.
I thought I was unlucky, but now that I've endured
and earned the passage out,
I understand what all this has been about.

Isn't poetry all about perfection?

No, no—poetry is all about mistakes.
The poem begins when it gets away
from you, begins to travel on its own
knocks open doors and cupboards at night

boards the wrong train
sleeps with the wrong man
or maybe accidentally
the right one
has sudden children
who are perfectly unpredictable in their early
or late arrival.

Poetry sits on the bed in a hotel room
naked (if poetry is honest, it comes into being naked
sometimes)
with two minutes before the taxi
scribbling these lines.

Three Surrealist Women and the Skins of an Orchestra
after Dali

By the suggestion of an ocean,
the rocks allow a passage.
Three women gather the skins
of the instruments used
to win their pinkish hue.
One appears empty-handed,
triumphant in her tatters.

One gently drapes the cello over her arms,
more like an offering than a child.
The oldest blends into stone,
holds the piano by a fingertip.
If she wanted, she could shake it like a sheet.
But for the moment, it lies like a puddle
in the sand. They gather round.

They might be about to fold things up for the night.
It is over. Or it might be about to begin.

Love-spinning

Our grandmothers, and theirs, if they knew
of this chance crossing, they'd be spinning too.

They'd wind our names together on their distaffs,
divining children we would never have

unless they spun, knowing our lives would turn
along the woof and warp of the slow burn

of their deft shuttles, weaving for our lives
to make one cloth. They'd leave the ends untied

so we could choose—as if there were a choice—
once we spoke, once the rhythm of your voice

met mine. Our bodies barely brushed that time
we met, and spoke, but when we said good night

I held that sound inside me like a child.

Carousel

This is a dance she doesn't understand,
the way these carousel swans swing round.
The wheel moves fast, directions change, shapes merge,
children shriek and name their wild birds names,
hooking their feet in small claw stirrups

She begins to think of her arms as having thousands
of small birdbones, the beginning of wings,
grounded only by the width of each bone—
And she begins to know how air can travel through
a body, lift it for a dance of skin and feather

grown light, and lighter, loosing itself to wind.

Kummerspeck

In our house, we've been keeping an eye
on the grief bacon this year.
I learned long ago that life is no pony farm,
but we can keep our *Ohren steif*, our ears stiff,
aware and hopeful, living out here
where the fox and the hare say goodnight
to each other, far from the rush of the city.
We try to keep tomatoes off our eyes,
and it helps to realize that some in power
don't have all the cups in the cupboard.

Some have eaten their wisdom with spoons
and are full, must always know best.
So now we have the salad
tossed further than we ever predicted.
Those playing the offended sausages fill the news,
one or another going for the *Extrawurst*,
which we have been trying to avoid in theory
and also on the table.
Too many only understand train station
and can't see another side.

I wish the *Angsthasen* would find a way
to jump over their fear-rabbit shadows
and think something new. I was warned early on,
if you give the devil your little finger,
he will take the whole hand.
Every morning in this time, we might
be trying *Friede, Freude, Eierkuchen*
(peace, joy, pancakes),
though we are still keeping an eye
on the grief bacon.

Changing Reality

New to this virtuality, I noticed another option,
a simple click to touch up appearance.
Why not—in these days when we could choose to change
so many things, even our background,
make up where we are and edit
ourselves. Maybe this was some new kind of filter.

But I wasn't expecting such a versatile filter.
Who knew a single extension would open one option
after another. Once I realized I could edit
my messy hair and work on my disheveled appearance,
I gave myself a haircut, with palm trees in the background,
and was eager to try other possibilities for change.

In the closed-in days, I began realizing I could change
almost anything, apply a different filter
to alter other things, not just those in the background.
Smoothing skin and muscle tone became an easy option.
With a click, I could improve the appearance
of the house, positioning perspective to edit

out anything we wouldn't want seen, edit
all the familiar arguments, effortlessly change
our idea of reality, not just the appearance.
I got rid of my glasses, added X-ray vision, could filter
away a few years or more, maybe even with the option
of doing them over, moving some issues into the background.

But seriously (without going into too much background),
the world really opened up when I discovered I could edit
the way others appeared, that I had the option
to adjust a reaction in the mind, start to change
a pre-programmed response to an issue, filter
the negativity, move past the immediate appearance

of a comment, a position. Behind an appearance,
there is always something less visible in the background.
I could see the possibilities of this multi-purpose filter
that could take a source of trouble and edit
past how something was said, choosing to change
how it was received. All around, an inspired option.

We could all use such a filter to see beyond appearance,
take the option to be kind, move history to the background,
edit how we see it, and open the way to change.

III

The Farthest Side

As you start to walk on the way,
the way appears.

—Rumi

The Farthest Side

Some afternoons, in the small space of time
between my coming home from school
and his heading off to work, second shift, and maybe
some of third (what did I know of those austere days),
my father would have a question waiting for me.
We couldn't usually find a way to get beyond
all the history that divided us, that kept us
far from each other, for such a small house.

But when I came home, he would sometimes
have the paper open to *The Far Side*,
usually one that went a bit further over the edge,
and would ask if I understood this one.
We had our dark favorites that were fairly clear.
The engorged snake stuck in the crib with the teddy bear.
The spider web at the bottom of the slide—
"If we pull this off, we'll eat like kings."
But the fact that he asked me, even back then,
about the more complicated ones, believing I would know
about natural selection, space, modern art or poetry
meant more to me than I would have admitted,
more than I even realized at the time.

When we talked about Cow Poetry, it went beyond
the cow's damning the electric fence. The pilots wondering
what a mountain goat was doing in that cloud bank ahead
brought us to the moment outside the frame.
Maybe Larson intended that a few of these,
like the meat in the bowl on the window table,
or Cow Tools, with its unrecognizable objects,
would resist any quick interpretation
and just get people talking.

The Typewriter

If I could write it by hand and turn it in, I did that,
though it wouldn't look as polished as others.
Many already had computers in those days.

Our old manual typewriter had a few keys stuck,
so the handed down electric one appeared
like a godsend at first,

until one significant catch revealed itself.
If a hand rested on the metal frame,
it would shock the user. Less than user friendly,

it sat on the far end of the dining room table, hulking
and too heavy to easily move, humming loudly,
a slight burnt smell when we plugged it in.

No door in the house to close, baby brothers making
a fort under the table, shooting pellets at my legs.
No kindred spirit pausing in the stairwell

at the prow of the house, listening to the typewriter
through a shut door, wishing his little starling
a lucky passage.

Just touch the keys, not the edge, and you'll be fine.
I wasn't good at keeping to the keys.
A pause to think or rest my wrist would mean

a shock that would find its way to this page.
It was what I knew, to come up against walls.
But with the wits to try again, I went with what I had,

and eventually I flew.
Resourceful, I found an always open room
in the cardio wing of the nearby hospital,

with state-of-the-art, non-shocking typewriters.
Empty in the evening, free coffee down the hall
for the third shift. I could type all night,

and sometimes, given the scope of my plans, but having
underestimated and procrastinated, I needed to.
Those high school years, I would ride my bike

the two miles home, pedaling fast to keep on
the headlight, sometimes at four in the morning.
If my teachers only knew the lengths I would go

to get it done on time, my latest project typed
on the high-grade paper, glowing in my backpack.
Having found the window to get through and finish it,

I would be soaring high, far outside of any walls,
flying through the deserted streets,
safe under the blanket of stars.

Pantoum on a Paper Moon

When it was make believe
I still believed in you.
This paper moon is all I have
to show for all those years

I still believed in you.
This song an early memory
to show for all those years
it seemed to speak directly to me,

this song, an early memory.
Watching the paper moon rise,
it seemed to speak directly to me,
the summer on that makeshift sea.

Watching the paper moon rise
is how I will remember you,
making summer on that shifting sea.
A circle back in time

is how I will remember you.
This paper moon is all I have,
a circle back in time
when it was make believe.

Circle in the Sand

When we get to the beach, we head down
close to the water, each of us carrying
a bucket full. Dad has the one stocked
with medicine—peroxide for cuts, kerosene
to take the tar off our feet, ammonia
for the jellyfish and man-of-war stings.
The summer days all blend into one,
though sometimes the water is as calm
as a lake and sometimes the waves are high,
towering to our small bodies.

He clears away the seaweed with a hoe
(we always bring a hoe) and makes a quick
clean place for us to play. And then he uses
the hoe to draw the circle. It's one of the first things
I remember—that circle. Big enough for all of us
and for all our buckets and shovels. If we want
to build separate castles, sometimes we ask
for the circle to be bigger.

Then they walk into the ocean and leave us to play
inside our circle. We never leave it. Each of us
watches out for the other. Mom and Dad go pretty far out
and swim and wave and it looks like they are smiling.
When one of our toys rolls out, we stretch to get it
but we always keep a foot in the circle, trying to reach the thing
we've lost—while staying within the rules.

One Early Morning

One early morning,
swimming just at sunrise,
I was surrounded by turtles, just hatched,
making their perilous way out to sea.
I didn't touch—but one by one they brushed
softly against my little girl body.

Planting Cape Florida, Key Biscayne

After the hurricane, I gave my students
extra credit to join in replanting the park.
I was one set of hands, but I could bring
a small fleet to the task.
Andrew had taken down so many trees,
but had mostly uprooted invasive species,
Australian pine and melaleuca, making room
for the native sea oats, the sea grapes
and gumbo limbo, for the hardwood hammock
of old Florida to grow its way back.
We planted near the lighthouse that had stood
through so much—war, fire, hurricanes.
We planted near the beach
where turtles have nested for generations—
where, one mid-summer evening years later,
I stayed with my family as late as we could,
a full moon rising at sunset.
One nest so close to the water, we worried
the tide would wash it away in the night,
when the sand in the nest suddenly stirred,
and the turtles emerged, one by one,
and then dozens all at once.

Old Florida would have already been gone
on the cape, if not for the park
that made it greener and open to all.
And maybe the hurricane that took so much
could also bring back the land in some places.
I thought of this on my knees in the earth,
in the early morning light, the linings of silver,
putting in tree after tree that my children would see,
decades later, growing taller every year.

Swamp Roses

People down here want to make roses grow,
trying new rounds of chemistry,
every kind of poison or solution
you can devise to make them bloom
uniform, cultivate them for a prize.

While the swamp roses come up wild,
and the hyacinth floats on the surface
of streams, with the blue forget-me-nots,
branches uncoiling as the flowers do.

Find me here instead
something that grows unforgettably blue,
the tiny wild garden you can see
growing in the crevices of rocks
or traveling like water down the river.

This Old Thing

Growing up in the South,
I watched one woman or another
spend the entire day making a cake,
to bring to the party *a little something*,
and play it down, as everyone
wolfed it down with praise.
My aunt spent weeks knitting a shawl
you could wear three ways,
a piece of art by the time she was done.
And when it was admired, I heard her say
Oh, this old thing?
I carry that answer with me to this day,
underneath it all, though I'd rather
be able to leave some of that behind,
the hesitation, still finding myself at times
quietly keeping it together
with a cake, a costume, a poem,
with this or that old thing.

Letters from La Paz

I. La Paz, Bolivia

What higher hillside could I ever find
to roll these poems down to where you are
listening for them each night under stars
and the growing moon, full in two days' time.
I can hear the children's voices echo
in the schoolyard. They sound like birds singing.
In this town, on market streets, you can find
wings of flamingos, fetuses of llamas
to be wrapped in silver paper for spells,
a thousand stories woven into cloths
the colors of birds, the pink of lovers,
the green always prayed for in these mountains,
in these songs, the textures of this hillside,
this mountain, this moon, rolling down to you.

II. Festival de la Virgen de Urkupiña, Cochabamba, Bolivia

Once every year in the heart of August,
the people throng to find the Virgin here,
to dance the devil dances in her name,
to climb *Kalbario* to crack off rocks
for luck, to read their fortunes in the lines
inside the split rocks, to find the figure
of the Virgin in the veins, map their lives,
their histories, their futures, to pile rocks
as altars, place their wishes, manifest
in paper money, toy trucks, dollhouses,
effigies of lovers, all in miniature,
carefully placed icons for miracles
and pour the *chicha* in the heart of rocks,
brought home in plastic bags to bless the year.

III. Cuzco, Peru

In the parade, dancers wear histories
over their shoulders and whirl in the streets,
dressed in Spanish moss or wrapped in the skin
of a mountain lion or the body
of a condor hollowed out to costume
a young boy—whose role is to move between
the dancers like a ghost, a spirit bird
between two worlds. He is learning English
in school. Sundays he goes to Catholic church,
and he lights a candle for his mother,
and he lights another for the condor
he will wear that Sunday like a body
wrapped around his secret voice—his heart passed
in skins, in feathers, scales, in human form.

IV. Isla del Sol, Lago Titicaca, Bolivia

The full moon is returning to the lake,
this half-heart shaped bay in this ancient sea.
Out of this half-circle window, the sky
turning flamingo pink in memory
of the birds that once filled the air with wings,
of ceremonies made to the sun's birth
and death at the birth of each moon. This one
will die soon. It has reached its fullest point
on this lake as big as a sea, this brief
moment, long as an hour, long as a life
spent where we can feel the shape of the earth
around us like a body, move with us,
like centuries move around these ruin walls
in streaks of sun and moon unchanged by time.

How They Arrived

Every storm tells a story, leaves a trail,
maps itself in the leaves and trunks of trees,
into every seed that makes a journey.

One thing grows within and out of another.

Orchids flowering by chance along
the fallen trees, or rising up the cypress
in random patterns, unlikely blossoms.

The trees in this strand were much bigger
one hundred years ago, before the storm
of the century pulled them from their soil,

scattering seeds that would grow into

these volunteers, who hold their orchids high,
as if they remember how they arrived
and the long journey they hold inside.

Recovering the Lost

Some things might best survive by being lost
or stolen, hidden, sunk beneath the waves,
for years preserved, tucked deep inside a chest.

Our art, sometimes by chance, escaped the past
by being shipwrecked early, to one day
be found, having survived for being lost.

Karyátides, stone women used as posts,
for years held up Acropolis like slaves.
The stolen one preserved, her face and chest

carvings still clear. Her sisters' features almost
disappeared, worn away by industrial rain.
Minoan island city-states survived, though lost

inside the ash that rained and spread across
the houses—still intact—forgotten ways
for years preserved inside the earth's deep chest.

Years later by that sea, a child will cast
and sink her dreams like stones. She's told they weigh
too much to keep. Will they survive those lost
long years, preserved, tucked deep inside her chest?

Library of Veria, Greece

We started with the maps,
the children's lines and colors charting a way
to think about the future and the past.
Earlier that day, we'd driven by the old factories
once used for canning peaches,
now full of people moving through,
but caught in the long still moment of a life
stalled, even in this frantic motion out and forward.
Some children drew a village in Syria,
a home they no longer knew.
Some—the place they thought they might be heading to.
Some had the past falling off the page,
as if the memories were fading too, that world closed
and now so far away, far from this sudden island
in the middle of a childhood.

The waters had monsters circling beneath.
The land was hazy, as if nothing yet existed,
the stories in the shapes imagining futures
past all this. I wished I could tell them
anything certain, how best to find the way.
But as a child of refugees whose own worlds
blew apart and hurled them elsewhere as children,
I have so much to say
and so much not to.
We have to hope this too shall pass
and we will pass
something kind here,
if even for a day.

A small place of refuge, the library,
in this world of dark-eyed Alexandria
who had drawn her map with a fire at its center,
but we won't go entirely there, not today,
though thinking of why these children are here,
the history—Alexandria—is not that far away.

The young cartographers finish with a flourish,
having imagined where they are heading,
drawing it closer into being.
They move with their papers to the front desk,
checking out books in a language they don't yet know
but are quickly learning, and they head out waving,
smiling for the moment
at the possibilities in their hands.

Learning to Breathe

I grew up holding my breath.
It was something I could do.
As a child, I could dive ten fathoms down
for that sand dollar
or something else that looked like treasure.
I could swim the length of an Olympic pool
and back underwater, and further,
always pushing it further,
training my lungs to let me stay longer.
In my home, I often felt I had no power,
but there was power

in being able to always push it further.

When I later learned to deep-sea dive
I had to go against
that inclination to hold my breath.
For me, there was significant adjusting,
as a body of water meant
to get down there and back up
in the short time that I had.
I had to learn to breathe steadily,
the main rule, never hold it.
At first, I had to say it in my mind—
Never hold your breath.

But once I learned, I loved belonging

to that world, while also being alien to it,
first through the wrecks on both coasts, then
volcanos under Santorini, looking for Atlantis,
and later the perspective from down under,

the side glance of the sea turtle appearing
on the barrier reef, gliding over its expanses
and losses.
Breathing steadily, adjusting carefully
to changes in depth, even back on land,
breathing, even in the surge of the unknown,
breathing, always remembering to

just keep breathing through it.

Haiku Petroglyphs

One winter morning
down Paseo del Volcan
trying not to speed

too quickly past ghosts
of others who have traveled
scribbling petroglyphs

on the face of rock
exposed like an expression
of dormant stirring

edges of rifting
deep faults where volcanos formed
the cinder canvas

sisters separate
nod to each other across
the ruptured time lines

scrawled within our cells
stick figures remembering
writing one story

Elemental Trail

Through thousands of light years, travel on,
making an album of the stars,
each image sent, already gone,
through thousands of light years—travel on,

recording the ancients, the long
elemental trail fused in ours
through thousands of light years, travel on,
our family album in the stars.

On Foot

after a line by Edith Södergran

On foot, I had to cross the galaxy.
I left without luggage or gear, knowing
nothing I had would be of use out there.
It felt long, but I can't say quite how long.
Time unfolds in space, and I soon realized
this wasn't the average pilgrimage.
I grew thankful for the unexpected

wormholes, useful to cover some distance.
I can't say what I needed to retrieve,
or even if, when, or where I left it.
It is a secret, kept even from me,
and frankly I'm not sure anyone will
believe this story anyway. At first,
I kept my path as far as I could from

the dark matter, though it was always there,
and I wished I could understand it more.
But once I recognized the energy
those expansions could release or create,
I knew I could take it back to the shore,
finding the swell of that particle wave
and all the light in the dark of deep space.

Southern Cross

It wasn't what drew me there,
but when I saw the Southern Cross
that year, visible all night down under,
turning with the hour,
it took me home, to my childhood
when I didn't quite realize
what had risen
just above the horizon,
but I knew enough to know
I could keep that starry kite
if even for a little while
up above the boundary line.

I didn't know it then, how special
the sighting was, my place in the world
far south enough to see it,
my hometown floating on the edge.
People looked right at the cross
and didn't seem to notice
it was there
before it dipped below again.
Almost like a secret, that made it mine.
It was something I could turn to,
away from all the trouble,
and call my own.

Outback

I was grown before I knew the moon
waxed and waned that way,
waxed in a D and waned in a C.
Since no one ever showed me,
I showed my children, probably
from the first time we looked at the night sky.

Though you might have known this scientifically,
sometimes you have to go to the other side of the world,
travel through the outback, feeling small again
and far away, before you discover the moon
waxes and wanes somewhere else
in the opposite way.

IV

Time in the Wilderness

I learned when I had young children that you can always do something.
If you can't do a poem, you can do a line. And if you can't do a line,
you can do an image—and that pathway that leads you along,
in fragments, becomes astonishingly valuable.

—Eavan Boland

The First Sea

The children are sorting the world of dreams
and speak of them in the morning, beginning to tell
the real from shadow. The story line blurred,
the edge of sleep and the wake of yet another storm.

We chart the world with every word we speak. I wish I could
tell them there are no monsters of the deep, but that is exactly
where to find them—in the fears swimming deep inside
the cells of our bodies, or spiraling, one around another.

The mind a sail, the bed a vessel ready to transform
a pirate ship, a submarine, the belly of a whale.
With each new word they learn, one more memory
will sink beneath the waves. Like swimming in that first sea,

that grew smaller and smaller, as they already found
ways to comfort themselves. On any morning,
I find my daughter has traveled to yet another
country, speaks a different language. Every dawn

her world is new. She dreams the same dreams I do.
She may be falling, falling, running, or unable to run
when she needs to. I can't protect her there.
We grow further away all our lives. Language drifts us

from those early waters, and our stories, long submerged,
swim up years later. So many of these moments,
each a small Atlantis, will be covered by the sea—
as language takes over, relegates the rest to dream.

Astronaut Training

I ate the applesauce.
—John Glenn, 1962

Nothing really prepares you,
though there are plenty of books on *what to expect*,
because on some level you are not in control.
The vomit comet gives you a clue
that things will be different.
The centrifuge spins you around faster and faster,
changing gravity.

Much of the preparation is in the mind,
how to handle the unexpected,
and there is always the underlying fear
that you might burn up on re-entry.
No matter what, nothing really prepares you.
The simplest of actions will become an event,
the small step, the first swallow of applesauce.
Thinking—Houston, we have a problem.
He didn't eat the applesauce.

Sixteen sunrises and sunsets pass
while others experience one night.
You might sleep hanging from the ceiling
and wish for earplugs so the rocket burns
don't wake you, but it is also clear
that out here—in zero gravity,
where the whole picture comes into focus,
your heart doesn't have to work as hard.

Birth Announcement

I could already hear you, even as you were emerging,
so quick you were to make your presence known.
But your father was the first to see you.

What does she look like? A mother's first question.
His answer unexpected, or perhaps somehow expected.
The things men say that they regret for their lives.

This man who adored you even before you were born,
this man who, months later, still gazes at your face,
and waits for every chance of a smile—

She looks like an internal organ, your father answered,
so startling that the nurse came running to my side
to reassure, to cover up his words in that moment,

and for the anxious mother, for all those present
in the room and the future, proclaimed it three times
She's beautiful. She's beautiful. Just beautiful.

Counting Two

Suddenly my son can count—
One. Twooo!
His one a calm, tame number.
His two a wild creature,
the vowel stretching limbs,
traveling continents, oceans,
taking on the world in its primordial twos.

Three, four, five? my practical parent self suggests.
One, he answers authoritatively,
and then, again, the wildly gestured *Twooo!*

One. Twooo!
He counts the flock of birds
One. Twooo!
The cars on a passing train
One. Twooo!
A march of ants. Drops of desert rain.

At night, exhausted from his exponential math,
his head against my heart,
counting beats perhaps
to fall asleep,
I fall with him,
thinking of his *Twooo!* his wildly gesturing hand,
showing me how well he understands—
my little son—
that two is so much more,
twice as much in fact,
infinitely more
than one.

Questions from Four Dimensions

How many hours are there?

Is this Planet Earth?

How far is outer space?

Are we real?

What's *your* secret identity?

So we should only tell lies on April Fools'?

If children are the future,
does that mean you are the past?

How do you make a table of continents?

Is that why grown-ups are grouchy—
because they've outgrown their lucky jackets?

Where is time, and how do we run out of it?

Giant Children

Are these the giant children that you teach?
my daughter asked me on the way in to a class visit.
I laughed, but only later thought

how we are all children of varying sizes
making mistakes all our lives.
With any hope, not the same ones over and over.

It helps toward forgiveness,
though one wonders how that is really possible
if there is no remorse.

It can take a long time to learn
that forgiveness is not the same thing
as condoning or allowing more harm.

There's a difficult balance,
and as I take the baby steps to figure it out,
I am in those woods again without a guide,

trying to find my way through,
while at the same time having to lead
others through the thicket of questions

and the answers I thought I knew.

Spaceship with Saint Giovannino

We had been pointing out the smallest details,
often on the periphery, Icarus falling,
nearly invisible, only legs left disappearing into the Aegean.
No one in that painting was watching it happen,
but here in this one, in the Palazzo in Florence,
the figure in the background shielded his eyes from the sun
to look up directly at the object.
A spaceship, my son pointed out. I turned
to look closer and correct him. This was the fifteenth century.
But there was the ship, in a spiral curve of light.

It went beyond a cloud or a star, this messenger,
such an unusual angel.

The spiral took me to the fresco from years before in Kosovo,
The Crucifixion, with two figures riding inside their stars
on either end of the wall above the altar.
There is a word we have given to what we can't
quite understand or explain, or to what separates us—
Ruth in tears amid the alien corn,
the way the stars shone alien and remote
that afternoon in the painting in the Palazzo,
then followed us into the evening
and all the way home.

Interplanetary Spelling Bee

What if you make it all the way to interplanetary?
　　—Dylan to his sister Christabel

For decades, we thought it was just static.
We could not discern any pattern, but over time,
we have learned that language is more
than sound waves. It could be intensities or colors,
distinctions far beyond the color/colour variation.

Now the static is standard in the spelling bee.
My daughter has advanced to interplanetary.
The participants are sponsored, but tickets for the family
cost an arm and a leg, or two tentacles. Depending.
She ends up near the front, in row 993,
but it is still hard for our limited eyes to see.
In the first round, 3,443.5 are eliminated.
A small percentage of the spellers.

The rules are similar—planet of origin, alternate pronunciation.
If a definition doesn't clarify, one might request
a representative object or interpretive dance,
like the green liquid moving in and out of an orb
that I still don't understand.

A few more rounds and the words heat up,
like the interpretive dances for *heartthrob*, and *combustible*.
We cross our fingers, and my daughter gets an easy one:
sesquipedalian. But she still asks for it in a sentence:
"It is hard to spell some sesquipedalian surnames."
In her school, she always has the most sesquipedalian last name, with nineteen letters,
but here, her name is fairly short and simple, in comparison,
easy to spell. The next word is on a frequency
my untrained ear can't even hear. The speller waves
an appendage and passes through with ease.

The beings with more than one head or collective minds
seem to do quite well. But in the end, they tend not
to win overall, possibly because they become overconfident,
or because there is always some infighting.

Or maybe because spelling is more than just collecting.
Sometimes it is feeling the form and tone of a word,
a language, and making it your own, even for a moment.
My daughter can make many words her own, and her mind travels
great distances. She even makes it to the final fifty
but is eliminated on a word with so alien a concept,
it is not sound, not color, not intensity.
There is no object or interpretive dance for this one.

The winner, still in the equivalent of middle school,
had studied on ninety-seven planets and had even visited
other dimensions. In fact, the bee organizers are considering
the idea of an interdimensional bee, but are discussing
the obvious problems, such as infinite homonyms,
infinite participants, which would mean infinite rounds,
even infinite versions of the same speller.
Infinity divided by any number is still infinity.

There is so much we still don't understand, so much
we haven't yet discovered, but we are fairly certain
that no matter how we try to bend time and dimension,
an interdimensional bee would simply have
no end

Living with Aliens

From the moment there is evidence
they are there,
they slowly take over our bodies.
We are sustenance, spaceship to arrive,
shelter while they grow, heart by brain by limb,
and when they emerge and show themselves,
they exert a mysterious force that makes us
fall completely under their power.
Everything they see is an unidentified object.
They stare at their own hands,
amazed they are attached. And probably useful.
They acquire the sense of object permanence,
though the years that follow may unravel and unlearn
some of this. They are already making plans,
asking questions that complicate our answers,

while our own language becomes stranger by the day
and over time, our clothes and music stranger by night,
and the curious item we used to read to them has become
an artifact from our own alien history.
We ask primitive questions that expose what we don't know
about the new wiring, make them laugh out loud
as we hold their technology upside down,
pretend we know what we are doing.
The exchange has been taking place for years.
They usually keep us too busy to notice.
But then, on some average day, maybe on waking,
the turn suddenly arrives in a red sky—
this is *their* world—the compass spinning in time—
and we step out that morning to meet the dawn
on an unrecognizable planet.

Zero Hour

Running late again at 6:00 a.m., the hardest thing
is getting them going, grouchy in the morning,
popping bagels in the toaster, last-minute
filling of forgotten field trip forms,
while thinking of the complicated day ahead,
one to zero hour marching band and two to early jazz,
three schools this year (only one magic year
when they all went together), looking for the
missing homework, the lost jacket,
the last pair of clean socks, just wear the dirty ones
(they said this would get easier),
packing lunches, snacks, and instruments,
the sax and tenor sax, the clarinet, trumpet,
and the flute, grateful for the piccolo and not a tuba,
helping with a backpack half the weight of my daughter
and the tennis, swimming, and cross-country bags,
rethinking all these activities, climbing in the car,
and the sudden question about more supplies
and if I'll have time—a posterboard, model magic,
acrylic paint, not to mention, a glue gun,
when is the project due—tomorrow?
well, today, but I can ask for an extension,
just barely here—maybe I'll get to work on time,
now that I'm in the final drop-off line, feeling proud of my
success—quick, run in, not a minute to lose—
Mom, we have to go back—I forgot my shoes.

High Noon at the Remote Corral

A scream from the back room, which usually means the internet died,
and I come running with a hotspot, hoping to bring it back to life,
all the late risers in town now online too, maybe working, but likely
just turning on Netflix, bank-robbing our bandwidth, but this time
it's a forty-five question test, completed on time only to be erased
by a keyboard shortcut, a lethal combination of Ctrl-P and Cancel,
while across the house, the bari sax making it clear that this homestead
is not big enough for dueling instruments, though we never realized
how far even the little flute carries in these competing classes,
and now another blue screen of death, the crashing websites not scalable
enough for this scale of new users, as the noon hour looms,
and trumpet starts having a showdown with Spanish, the parents always
asking—*Are you muted?*—as nearly appropriate expletives erupt,
forgetting the day of the accidental unmuting of *This is so boring*,
accidentally evaluating the poor teachers who are trying their best,
class chats rolling in out of sync, the whole rhythm of learning out of sync,
the house a machine for many months now, whirring in all corners,
and worrying about the system giving an F until an item is graded
(as if we needed more stress), and now the youngest moving to the porch
for P.E. and maybe some stress relief, doing line dances with no line,
it only dawning on him yesterday that this dance is usually done
with others, hence the meaning of line dance, while back inside,
another child left behind in the tunnel (or is it a collapsing mineshaft)
between the meet and the breakout room, while I try to appear
on my own screen at noon, looking calm and having it all under control,
trying to arrange as much asynchronous as possible, which thankfully
works well for these classes, since when I do unmute, there is usually
a trumpet, sax, clarinet, flute, piano, or one nearly appropriate curse
or another in the background, waving in meetings, smiling at
some heads that I am sure don't understand—and I don't complain
anywhere except maybe in this poem, having learned to be thankful,
always thankful that things aren't worse, however worse they get,
in this new world where what worked yesterday might not necessarily
work tomorrow, and then one I haven't heard before, but it seems
about right, a holler from the kitchen table announcing—*I can't see
anyone else on screen anymore, but now there are hundreds of me.*

Finding Home

(four tanka)

When the days closed in,
we followed the arroyo
behind our house, crossed

to the high desert forest,
took the trails in the foothills.

Juniper, piñon,
a pair of spotted towhees,
the owl calling out,

the light on the Sandias
changing, turning with the Earth.

Time still unsettling,
children schooling underfoot,
but something shifted.

Together on this planet,
we still find ourselves alone.

We can view this time
and space as isolation
in the universe

or we can see what we have,
find the paths that call us home.

Under the Lawrence Tree

The summer night cool on our skin, the colors
fading quickly into evening. Together here,
we grew into the Sangre de Cristo skies.
My children born and rooted in this place,
it became home, waiting for the hummingbird,
watching the lizard disappear into the dusk.
Like Lawrence, fellow traveler, they can see
the tiny dinosaur that darted into his poem.

This land held me when I thought it was over,
brought me back, showed me another way to go,
took me to this time, lying here on our backs
with new eyes. Poets, artists, children—
tilt the world, our view to the branches
and through to the stars.

Short Subjects with Long Titles (Epigrams on Art, Poetics, and Philosophy)

Three-year-old Christabel, on her mother asking, "What are you girls talking about in the middle of the night?"

> It's not the middle.
> We're talking in the back of the night.

Six-year-old Alexander explains irony to five-year-old Aria, after Aria's yelling wakes the baby up and their parents say "Thanks a lot, Aria" and Aria answers "You're welcome!"

> Aria, they don't mean thank you.
> They mean you did something bad.
> It's another way of saying it.

Three-year-old Dylan, on his siblings teaching him to write his name correctly

> It's *my* name.
> I can write it any way I want.

Five-year-old Aria, on hearing the new Sewanee siren and announcement "Severe Thunderstorm with High Winds Approaching. Take Cover Immediately!"

> Time to fly kites!

Six-year-old Alexander, on hearing his mother and father argue about communication, his father's tendency to say "Uh huh" to everything, and his mother's asking "Uh huh? What does that mean?"

> Mommy, Uh huh means yes.
> It's a different language.

Four-year-old Christabel, offering an explanation about her horse

It's a pretend horse.
But I'm pretending it's real.
The Mommy horse is going off to write on her computer.

The children measuring the world by idiom and a few arms

How far is arm's length?
How far is that?
How long an arm?
Their arm? Your arm?
Or both?

The morning after our visit to the Museo del Prado in Madrid where five-year-old Dylan was fascinated by the monstrous figures in Hieronymous Bosch's "Garden of Earthly Delights"

Last night I dreamt about monsters.
Good thing I like monsters.

Four-year-old Aria, early seeker, looking intently at the Bible

This is a very big book.
I'm trying to find God in here.
It's G-O-D, right?

Three-year-old Dylan explaining the need for conflict in five-year-old Christabel's game

But there are always bad guys in princess games.

Aria and Christabel, early feminist critics, discuss the books Alexander is reading

> Those are boy stories. There are no girls.
> Except for the ones getting rescued.

Dylan, meaning to say "invincible," discusses a fellow first-grader

> He kicked me because
> he thought I was irresistible.

Christabel and Aria talk about their doll that was lost for a while

> Hey, Rapunzel's shoes still fit.
> It's a doll. Dolls don't grow.
> But shoes grow. They grow smaller.

The children after overhearing another discussion about work

> Mommy's work at the university is so hard.
> Now they want her to be a chair.
> A chair? What?
> Are they going to sit on her?

Christabel and Alexander interpret a work of abstract art

> Is this toddler art?
> Maybe it's a roller coaster.
> Or a treasure hunt.
> It could be stairs.
> Or nothing.

Four-year-old Dylan asking about different holidays

> When is the end?
> Is the end a holiday?

Four-year-old Aria, during our nightly ritual of poems, story, song and come back for a secret and another story, as she puts it—from her brain—on being asked by her tired mother to make it a very short story tonight

> Aria was walking through the forest.
> No animals.
> The End.

Time in the Wilderness

To hear it, we have to
be there, over time

tune an ear to the song
sparrow at sunrise,

the great horned owl at dusk,
reminding us

not to miss the trees
for the theory of the forest,

turning an old saying
around a child's observation,

the simplest question
opening the world again.

BIOGRAPHICAL NOTE

Diane Thiel is the author of eleven books of poetry, nonfiction and creative writing pedagogy, including *Echolocations*, *Resistance Fantasies*, and *The White Horse: A Colombian Journey*. Thiel's work has appeared in many journals, including *Poetry*, *The Hudson Review*, *The Hopkins Review*, *The Sewanee Review*, *The Dark Horse (Scotland)*, *Rattle* and *Prairie Schooner*, is reprinted in over sixty major anthologies, and has been set to music and translated widely. She has received numerous awards, such as the PEN Translation Award, the Robert Frost Award, the Robinson Jeffers Prize, the Nicholas Roerich Award, and she was a Fulbright Scholar. Thiel's translation of Alexis Stamatis's novel, *American Fugue*, received the NEA International Literature Award. Fluent in several languages, Thiel received her undergraduate and graduate degrees from Brown University and has taught English and creative writing for over twenty-five years. Originally from Florida, she is a Regents' Professor at the University of New Mexico and Associate Chair of the Department of English. She lives in Albuquerque, in the foothills of the Sandia Mountains. With her husband, Costa, and their four children, Thiel has traveled and lived in Europe, South America, Asia, and Australia, working on literary and environmental projects. For more information, please visit her website: www.dianethiel.net